Cristina Balau

ZOE

Sibiu, 2023

0

She felt as if everything had been erased, as if nothing was really as

she had remembered it.

As though her marks had never remained on him,

As if he had never been on her.

Chapter 1

After an unusually hot beginning of spring, so hot that I frequently felt as though I couldn't catch my breath, that night I was, finally, a little bit cold. Happy as I was though, I also kind of missed the hotness of the last few days. I was getting out of my new apartment, in a very quiet little neighborhood, just longing for a breath of fresh air. The moving had been exhausting.

It was for the first time that I was living alone and the thought of it scared me. As a consequence, my mind would just so often go back to my childhood, when everything was simple and my world was all about the books I'd be reading. I never realized how much I would be missing those moments in the future, until they hit me right in the face. 'I'll read more', I used to lie to myself, but never had the time.

I didn't know the neighborhood very well, so my feet just danced a little on the steps of the building and I let them lead the way.

Walking along the peaceful streets, apple trees and spring flowers would pave the road ahead, showing me the way. The sun was about to set, and a soft breeze caressed my purple silky blouse, tickling my soul.

Gazing in the distance, I saw him. He was wearing a blue shirt, a little rumpled, something so typical of him, I would later learn. Tall, mysterious, he was heading towards me. When only a few steps were left between us, I nervously straightened my back and hoped we would lock eyes. 'What is going on with me?', I thought.

My heart was beating so strongly, I presumed he couldn't have heard it and would stop to ask me whom was it beating for. When less than a meter was separating us, I felt as if the time had slowed down for a couple of moments. That man, which i felt I had seen before, in another life maybe, smiled at me, just a little, with the corner of his beautiful, full mouth. I answered back, blushing.

For a brief moment, when he passed by me, our hands touched, and I felt a thrill crossing my body. I wanted him to stop and kiss me. What a peculiar feeling, to want so much a man I had only seen once in my life. I turned my head after him, but all I could see was a shadow floating further and further away. My heart started beating insanely again and confused my mind. Sometimes, life is all about moments like these. Fleeting moments like the fuzzy 'luck' you see in the hot summer air, right before sunset. An arm reaching you, a good word coming at the right time and our entire existence would choose another track. I knew that. We had gathered together, in that unexpected moment, all the unspoken words.

...

For the rest of the night, our encounter was the only thing I could think about. His touch had left me such a familiar feeling, and an intense lavender perfume had followed me all the way back home. Where in time was that crooked smile taking me?

Mountains of boxes and bags were patiently waiting their turn all around me, in the small apartment. In an attempt to forget about the mystery man at least for the next hours, I chose, not at all random, a big box with the words 'unread books'. One by one, I read their titles and the summary, and I placed each one carefully on the shelf. As I was advancing with my little project I couldn't help myself from thinking how good it would be if I'd be this organized in other aspects of my life.

When I'd finally had enough with the unpacking, I left on the nightstand the last book from the third box I'd opened and went to the kitchen to boil some water. I loved to spend my evenings looking out the window, with a hot tea by my side. It was the best moment for my inspiration to kick in and often enough I would manage to write a few words down in the notebook I would intentionally let on the window. It was a habit I had taken on many years ago, during a time when in my writings you would frequently find as a dominant theme the perfume of orange peels and steamy tea.

I infused a handful of herbs and forest fruits from a tiny, transparent jar and, after what appeared to be a never-ending search, I found a knife I used to slice an orange. I abandoned the cup on the kitchen table and I lay down on the floor, where soon I would put a mattress and then, hopefully in the near future, a real bed. The thought at the beauty my apartment would be once everything would be in place, the perfume of the tea, the tiredness, combined with the vivid memory of the sensation the man I'd met earlier had given me made me fall asleep right there, laying on the floor.

Chapter 2

I was running towards him, as if my feet were made of steel. I was moving with difficulty while the ghost in front of me was gradually disappearing. As the tension between us was raising, the desire of seeing his eyes was more intense. I imagined they were blue and green and that the entire sense of the world was hidden in them. Drained of all power and breathing heavily, I sat down on the sidewalk. After a couple of moments, a touch took me by surprise.

- Are you ok?, he asked with a huskiness in his voice, hidden in the darkness of the night.

I felt that if I said anything in that moment, I would ruin everything. I wished I could read his every thought through those eyes that, even though I could not see them, I knew they were too full of light for my dark world. I was confused. How could I fall in love with something I had never seen? Resigned to the thought that he would never let me look at him the way I wanted to, I just stood there, petrified, under his heavy hand. I took a deep breath and smiled.

- Your touch is enough for me, for now, I told him and just like in a dream, I felt him smiling too. I didn't look up, but I knew.

A soft rain wet our thoughts. The drops would break the silence around us, and my heart beats started to calm down.

I woke up shocked by the impact a stranger could have had on me. It had been a long time since I'd dreamt so intensely. I rubbed my eyes a few times, just to be sure I was fully awake, I got up from the floor, put the tea to heat up again and started looking for my notebook in the mountains of luggage. I had to write. I put down on paper my dream, as detailed as I could. Taking out of me by writing everything I thought or felt in a certain moment was a habit that calmed me every so often, especially when every other activity seemed to fail.

Oh! That annoying whistle! The tea boiled over, interrupting my train of thoughts in the middle. I poured it back in the mug, took out a blanket from a box and went out on the balcony. I was starting work at my new job, and I was excited. I had wanted for so long to work at that radio station, and I knew I had to give everything I had and then some for my new boss to be impressed with me and sign my contract for an undetermined time. This was what I had learned for, this was the reason I had suffered at all my other jobs, for years and years, making coffee and earning too little. It was my chance to do exactly what I had wanted all along.

With this thought in mind, I took a sip of tea, abandoning the mug by the window. It was too late, and I hadn't bought light bulbs for the apartment, so I closed the notebook and put it back somewhere in the luggage. I went out on the balcony one last time and watched the motion in front of the building. A few children had abandoned their bikes in front of another building. Two of them were laughing out loud, with their hands on the bellies, because of something the third one had said. The latter was acting like a little monkey, to keep his friends entertained. While he was fluttering his hands up and down, like a bird, his ice cream, which he kept in his mouth the whole time, had started to melt, leaving stains all over the kids' shirt, and one drop fell on his face and got in his nostril, making him choke a little, to his friend's amusement. A few blocks down, a young man was smoking a cigarette, alternating the smokes with a sip of some colored beverage. He was gazing in the distance. Our eyes met for a moment, and I smiled. His lips tried to form a smile back, without much success, and then he moved his eyes away. I kept watching him for a few more moments, pondering over what could have disrupted him on such a mellow evening, filled with children laughter.

My attention was diverted when, from the apartment from upstairs, I started to hear some movement, a sign that my new neighbors had arrived home. I had seen them every now and then, while checking the work at the block. They must have been double my age. They would always hold hands and go on long walks in the neighborhood, discovering everything like they would see it for the first time. They never got out of things to say to each other, she would laugh a lot, and he would run his fingers through her black, long hair every chance he'd get. When I heard again her colorful laughter, I couldn't stop myself from smiling imagining her in his arms, in the balcony, while they were watching the last rays of sun hiding behind the mountains.

I loved spending my time watching my neighbors and creating scenarios in my mind about what could be happening in every apartment, like in a book in which all the characters are equally as important. I would come up with situations and life stories, write them in my window notebook, and transform them in novels.

I fell asleep late, but Lale made sure I would wake up early. At 6AM I was up, my coffee was steamy and perfumed and I was walking around the house, half still asleep, with the mug in my hands. I had to get ready for my last round of baggage I had to bring home from my parents, but I couldn't gather the heart to go over there.

...

A few hours later, back to the building that would soon become my 'old home', I felt hopeless, the only feeling I didn't anticipate having in the midst of my leaving. It had been my childhood home; it was where I had cried out all my sorrows and had written my first stories. It came so much harder for me to leave my parents and I was afraid that in the end I would forget my mother's perfume from the rare moments when she would hug me and my dad's jokes whenever he'd see me under the weather.

In that moment I promised myself I wouldn't let my new life record over the memories of my last one.

Chapter 3

The first day of work. I chose a white blouse I had bought for the occasion and a tight skirt that annoyed me immensely because I had to pull her down every other step I'd take. I knew that would happen, but I wanted to look nice at least in my first day. After I'd get accustomed with the colleagues and the workplace, I would go back to my best outfits - jeans and a shirt.

Nervous and with an almost impossible to handle migraine, I stopped in front of the building and watched it for minutes. I had arrived much earlier, which was no mistake, because I knew I would panic before I entered the radio for the first time, officially. I analyzed the big entrance, made of two sliding doors, with logo of the radio above them. Then I took the windows one by one, the colors of the rooms from the first floor, the people moving on the halls and in the offices. I even thought for a second that I saw… no, it was not possible. I shook the idea out of my head and a few locks of hair tickled my nose and I sneezed. I took a deep breath and made the first step. And then the second one and another one after that. I kept the pace until I stepped into the building. 'From here you can only go forward', I told myself and held my head high.

I passed with flying colors the first minutes of smiling to everyone, I gave thanks for every 'Welcome' and, of course, I complied with the curiosity of the ladies from the second floor, who I already knew were the gossipers of the group - the girls from HR, Ana and Ileana.

- So where did you say you were from?

- Um… I'm from here.

- And? Are you married?

- No.

- Engaged?

- Also no.

- How old are you?

- 30.

- Oh, no problem then. We also have a friend who's still not married and she's your age. She's a good girl, she's not sad because of it. Just taking every day as it comes, right, Ileana?

I chose not to engage in the conversation anymore, because I felt it was very degrading for single women, so I just smiled lightly, said goodbye, and went in search of the kitchen. I needed a cup of coffee. Of course, I got lost on the halls of the newsroom. My old job had only a few rooms, all on the same floor, so a whole building was a little too much for me. Eventually, on the third floor, just as I got out of the elevator, I felt the unmistakable perfume of fresh coffee and I let it guide me to the kitchen.

The coffee pot that already been captured and I narrowed my eyes trying to discover who the thief was. When he felt my presence and faced me, for a moment my legs stopped listening to me. He was the man from my dream, the one I'd met the other day, randomly, on my street. The one who'd touched my arm in passing and had left a redness and a tremor. What was he doing here? Too many thoughts and too little time to answer all the questions because he was looking at me equally as intrigued. And a smile appeared in the corner of his mouth, I instantly started looking down at my shoes, just to avoid his eyes. I was ready to run out of there as fast as I could.

-   Do... I know you from somewhere?

-   Yesterday, on the street, was everything I could say.

-   Yes, I remember that. But I feel that maybe we know each other deeper. No? Well then, maybe it's all just in my mind. Anyway, I'm Andrew.

-   Zoe.

I managed to look into his eyes for the first time since he'd turned to look at me, holding the coffee pot. I'd wanted to tell him it wasn't just in his mind, that I felt your closeness too. But he was, nevertheless, just a stranger. I was contempt with just gesturing towards the fact that he was standing between me and the coffee.

-       Please, allow me!

He poured coffee into a cup, then some milk and a teaspoon of sugar, whilst looking at me the whole time, as if he was trying to guess the way I like my coffee just from the expression on my face. He then offered me the cup, slightly touching the tips of my fingers, and then he just left, leaving me standing there, in the middle of the kitchen, with a cup of coffee in my hand and a lost smile on my face.

Ileana finally found me, took my hand with a surprising friendly grasp that brought an unexpected joy in me, so I just left myself carried. She kept asking me a lot of questions, tireless and always smiling, and after half an hour, in which time she had offered me the tour of the building and showed me the best places for quiet breaks, and also where she hid her sweets and the best coffee, we already knew everything about one another. Both left-handed, both smokers, both dreamers. I liked very much this new friend of mine who had insinuated herself into my life without me having anything to say about the matter. And I didn't even know just how much I would count on her support in the near future.

She was also the one who told me that Ana was, from many points of view, our opposite. Quiet, lost in space, a young woman with the hair like fire and amazing curls, you would most often find her in one of Ileana's hiding spots, with her face behind a book, each week a different one. She was especially warm and got often lost in crowds, that's how quiet she was – something that she loved about herself. She could hide without trying too much and take care of her own thoughts.

For the rest of the day, the two girls helped me get accustomed with the equipment, my new microphone and the maze-like halls. The rest was poetry. The headphones, the solitude, the peace in the studio. On Air I would go only the next week, after I had watched and learned for a few days everything there was to know. I was to excited that most of the times I could be seen in the studio or in front of it, looking on the big separating window. I couldn't believe I was here, again.

I left the office very late in the night. I watched the sun set from the terrace at the last floor of the building, while having a smoke. The sun was so tender that I felt it, while it was preparing to hide behind the mountains, as it was caressing me gently. And I grinned back, leaning on a side of the terrace, while feeling the sun's warm embrace.

Soon enough, the HR girls joined me, and we talked and talked until almost midnight. Ileana laughed a lot, loudly, at anything, while Ana was never fully there, in our conversations. The two had known each other for many years, they were college roommates and when they took their degrees, they decided to do everything together from that point on – job, kids, life. They already had the job, and Ana had found her prince charming, so she felt entitled, without any trace of meanness, to encourage every woman she met, just as she had done with me when we met. This annoyed immensely Ileana, especially given the fact that she was also single and, being Ana's best friend, she had to hear about it more than anyone. `Come on, Ili, you'll see that you'll find someone`, Ana used to tell Ileana so often that the latter felt the urge to sow her friends mouth shut and just leave her be.

They called me Zozo and I loved it, because it reminded me of my childhood. The nickname stuck and, even thought it later spread in the whole radio, I only smiled when I heard these two geese call me that. And him, of course.

Chapter 4

It was the fourth night I'd wake up sweating incontrollable, just a few minutes after midnight. The nights were the hardest for me, because I felt it was the time of day when I would most lose control. And the fact that I didn't have anyone to call when I had these episodes made me feel that maybe it would be better for me not to sleep at all. `If I'd at least have nightmares`, I thought. Instead, I would just wake up scared to death, sweating, with one hand over the other, both of them over my heart. I would be venting, my vision was blurry, and my heart felt like it was trying to leave my body, that's how hard it beat. Sometimes I would think that if I took even for a second my hands away from my chest, my heart would for real run away, altogether with its arteries.

Most of the times, Lale wasn't disturbed by my insomniac nights, but the last ones had managed to also affect him. He would sit by my side, and for as long as my heart would beat at full speed, he wouldn't stop purring. I would pat him with one hand, while the other I used to try and soothe my anguish, playing with a strand of hair until, the much-expected moment would come when I would take my mind off the panic attack and I could finally concentrate on my breathing.

After a long time of having someone by my side in the bad nights, when I felt it could be better not to life at all than to life like this, now I was forced to get through this all on my own. And I was hard as hell. Everybody used to tell me that in time it would get better, but I just felt it was getting worse. Sometimes I thought how calming it would be to just take some pills and sleep for at least a few hours. But I didn't even know that scared me more – that I would take more than I should and I wouldn't wake back up, or that I wouldn't take enough and I would have to go through another panic attack.

I soon managed to calm down and I moved, with Lale by my side, on the balcony, waiting for the sunrise. The moment when the first rays colored the sky in warm pastels was one of my favorites. I would look at the way the apartments would lighten one by one, sleepy faces would smile to one another, numb bodies would hug as if they wanted to sleep together for a little more, the bread would loudly jump out of the toaster and the perfume of the coffee would cross the street and find me waiting for it on the balcony.

Half an hour later, the apartments would sink again into the darkness and the neighbors would happily wave at me while heading to work. I would smile back at them, acting as if I had just woken up.

Finally, I left the cat sleeping in the chair next to me and poured some water in the coffee pot. I made an omelet and took a long, hot shower. And then I chose the clothes for work and turned on the TV, not to watch something necessarily but more just as a back sound. I always felt, in the morning after a crisis, lighter, but convalescent. I needed a little time to get back on my feet, and this little ritual helped me.

I looked long at myself in the mirror and I tried on a smile. And then another one and another after that – until finally, inevitable, a real smile wrinkled the corners of my eyes and I felt like I was ready for a new day.

Chapter 5

The days went by easier since I'd restarted my radio journey. That is why I would spend most of my time at the studio; I just couldn't stay away – not from the radio, not from Andrew. The moments when we would meet, not random at all, in front of the coffee machine, were the ones when I would put on my most honest smile. He was the star voice of the radio. He'd come in the morning for his three hours of broadcast and then, instead of leaving and coming back in the afternoon when he would go live again, he'd prefer sometimes to just stay in the studio and help our colleagues or, funnily enough, cause mischief during the broadcasts, making faces in front of the huge window that separated the studio from the technical room, always causing a laughing fit in the middle of the news bulletins.

Most often we would meet by the coffee pot, and he'd always make me fight for it. He would ask a lot of questions about me that I had to answer to win a sip of coffee and again a set of questions for the milk and sugar. He was fascinating and interesting, even though he wouldn't talk much about himself. He just wanted to listen.

Still, something felt off about him. I would often catch him looking at me, smiling, but whenever I would smile back, he'd get serious and look in the other direction. I felt wanted and rejected by him at the same time. I'd started thinking that maybe these unexpected changes hid a secret bigger than he led on, with his mysterious attitude that I used to think was just part of his charm.

...

I didn't really feel like going out that night, but I also didn't want to disappoint my colleagues, who had been annoyingly asking me out for a while. In the end though, a glass of cognac at a terrace, in a surprisingly chilly night in the middle of summer, didn't sound that bad. I opened the closet and grabbed the first dress I could find - white, tailored to the body and with long, slightly billowy sleeves. I let my hair down, because I was having one of those rare days when my curls were soft and defined.

Andrew was again wearing a slightly wrinkled shirt, this time yellow, a perfect shade for his olive complexion. When he noticed me, he smiled broadly and walked towards me.

He pointed me towards the bar with his eyes, so I followed him without a second thought. The only two empty chairs seemed to be waiting for us, curious about the stories we were about to tell each other. I would find out that night that my bosses had fallen in love with his voice, two years ago. During that time, he was working for a newspaper in Bucharest and, through a series of fortunate events, ended up voicing a piece of news for the radio. The feedback was amazing. They wanted to hire him full time, offer him a show and a news anchor on the side. All for just 30 seconds of him talking about something he didn't even know what it was. He accepted immediately. The truth is, he had a golden voice.

A few hours later, I realized I'd had a little too much to drink, so I decided to go home. When he entered my cab, on the other door, I was taken by surprise.

-    Let's go, he said, and I started laughing.
-    Go where? I'm going home.
-    That's not possible! Wherever you'll go, I'll follow, so the decision is yours. We either go together at the club or home.

In that moment I could have let him at the club and be on my way home. I could have got out of the car with him, stayed for a cigarette and then made myself scarce. I had a million other possibilities apart from the one I chose, the wrong one… I had no reason to encourage this bond, even more so, I should have avoided it. Unfortunately, in that moment I didn't know this.

- The decision is yours, stop waiting. What do you want to do?

Something convinced me to take him home. I don't remember much from the road home, except a sense of familiarity. I felt that his place was there, beside me. In front of the block, we stopped and looked at each other in silence. There were no words left. I invited him, with a wave of my hand, to follow me inside.

He slammed down on the mattress I had placed on the floor and for a second I thought he wasn't well. Is if he'd read my mind, he answered with a slight nod of the head – everything was ok. He invited me to sit next to him, which I did. I covered him with a blanket and rest my head on a pillow, close enough to see his face in the light coming through the open balcony door. He was smiling.

- Tell me something about yourself.

I froze. What could I possibly tell this man who, through a series of strange occurrences, had arrived in my bed, more than what he had already made me tell him, at our coffees in the newsroom?

- How can you still talk with that alcohol-free diction? And what a beautiful voice you have, he kept telling me every couple of minutes. Even though he couldn't see my face, I am sure he knew that my cheeks were the color of freshly picked tomatoes.

-   It's a particularity of mine, I answered. The more I drink, the more correctly I speak.

We laughed a lot, about the way he was mumbling, about the night that had just passed, about the fact that we were together, on my mattress.

-   What a coincidence, I said, smiling.
-   It could be. But does anybody believe in coincidences anymore?

Subtly, the laughter stopped, and he looked at me, serious, as if he had just had an epiphany. For the first time I felt that he'd seen me. Not just then, in the light of the headlight outside the block, but for the first time since he had known me. I was shaking with exhaustion, so he pulled me closer to him and covered me. I forgot to breathe for a moment. It felt so good to be there, next to his heart. Too good.

I wished I could get up and leave, because something inside me told me that what was about to happen was wrong, but how could something that felt so good be wrong? Our first kiss was as unexpected as was the whole night. In that moment I didn't even realize that it had happened. I was ashamed, so I turned my back at him. I couldn't even look at him. And not because I felt bad for what I had allowed to happen, but because I wished too much for it to happen again. He read my mind again and turned me around to face him.

- I was always curious about you – were the only words he told me before kissing me again; tight, passionately, clutching me to his chest as my left cheek rested in his warm hand.

I kissed him with a strange longing, as if our lips had loved each other before, in a distant past, and now they'd remembered how good they felt together.

We stood there for a while, hugging. Even though I avoided his eyes, I could feel him following my every gesture. The only thing I could think about was that he would leave soon, and the next day everything would go back to normal. When he got up, I took his face in my hands and looked at him closely. I wanted to etch in my mind the portrait of the man who tied his heart to mine for one night.

On the doorstep he mimicked my gesture from earlier, then pressed his lips to mine three times, short and tight. He looked at me one last time from the stairs and then disappeared. I ran to the balcony and followed him as he was getting further and further, up until the moment when he disappeared again at a street corner.

...

I woke up the next day, sure that everything had been a dream. I wasn't possible, I reckoned, that it had just all happened to me. So, I decided that it wasn't real.

The hiss of the kettle took my thoughts away and I went into the kitchen to make my coffee. When I went back in the bedroom, I almost dropped the hot cup – I remembered everything vividly. His face between my palms, the smile at the corner of the mouth, the hotness of the cheeks and the press of his lips against mine. Everything had really happened. It really had. And if I still had a shadow of a doubt, when his name appeared on my cell, had last drop vanished. I could hardly persuade myself to answer it, and when I finally did, there was nothing but a small, almost inaudible sigh on the other end of the call. He was embarrassed.

- Are you ok?
- Yes, I answered, uneasy.
- Look… I must apologize. Last night I wasn't myself. I don't know what happened. If I made you feel bad, please forgive me.
- Well, if you'll apologize, then I must do it too, I replied.
- From what I remember, you were perfect.

The last line came with a softness in his voice that made me imagine him smiling. I smiled back. He hung up with a promise that the next time we met he would be good and not bother me again. I said goodbye secretly thinking that I wished that, just once, he would bother me a little more, if it meant I could feel his arms around me again.

Because everything had happened on a Friday, I had plenty of time to analyze each moment. I decided I would spend the next 48 hours doing… nothing. I went from the bedroom to the kitchen, then on the balcony and then again in the bedroom, until my coffee got cold, the sun set, and I could see again the sweet light of the lantern that had shielded us the night before.

For a few moments I played with the shadow he had left behind when he kissed me goodbye. I took it from the hallway, walked it through all the rooms and then went on the balcony and put it where I wished it could be him – on the armchair that was always empty. I sat on the other one and told the shadow everything I never wished for anyone to know about me, maybe not even himself, the real one. I imagined him smiling softly, thinking I'm just a child that loses herself in detail, in the body of a woman he was still curios to discover.

...

The next day I spent a few hours on the balcony, reading. A knock on the door woke me from my daydreaming. I walked, bored and stiff, towards the source of the noise. Through the peephole I saw him, fretful and with a bottle of wine in his hand. Wow. Twice in one weekend?

- What are you doing here?
- Well, I was thinking that maybe, I don't know, you wanted to talk. On Friday I was under the influence of alcohol, but it was such a pleasure being with you that I think now, in broad daylight, I would like it even more.

I chose not to say anything anymore and just make space for him to enter the apartment. He passed me, slightly caressing my cheek, without looking at me. We sat at the kitchen table. Neither of us had the courage to say anything, so I got up and searched for the bottle opener. I found it fast and opened the wine which I poured, my hands trembling, in two cups. Surely, the glasses were somewhen in the boxes, but I was scared that I would break them with my uneasy hands.

- What are you thinking about? he asked, and I blushed instantly. Because I didn't answer he continued: Look, I'll start. I'm thinking that our little date here is a little weird. I must admit that I'm feeling a little uncomfortable, but I'm sure this will pass soon. You?

-       I feel the same way, I answered smiling, and I took a sip of wine.

We talked about ourselves, our families, teenage years, and our meet cute. He confessed to me that he felt something strange, an almost unnatural closeness, and I was happy to be able to share with him that I felt the same way.

I told him about how as a teenager I took a course on radio even though at school I was learning math and physics. Despite my inclination towards mathematics, a subject in which I excelled, the artistic side of life always brought me greater satisfaction. So, during breaks I would always be listening to some radio station and imagined how it would be for me to be the one in everybody's headphones. The radio course came as such a blessing, a sign from God, and convinced me that this was what I was meant to do. But even so, I was rejected by every radio station I tried to work at, during college years. Until I got to the one that opened my way to the radio in Bucharest.

I then told him about my family and about the brother that I had lost when I was just 10 years old, but whom I'd always missed, even though I couldn't remember much about him. Lucas had been very ill and, when he died, my parents almost didn't survive his loss. I remembered my father never being there and my mother always crying in their room, grasping at his chest my brother's favorite toy. Years later, when I went back to those moments, I understood that my father had left the country and what kept my parents together was the fact that my mom never gave up on him – she would seldom send him letters, alongside photos stained by tears - `2nd of May, Zoe is 11 today. Next to her, Bea, her new friend`, was one of the annotations that stuck in my mind, because the photo was also vivid in my memory - me with my left hand around the shoulders of a girl about the same height as me, with dark hair, bangs so long they almost covered her eyes, both of us smiling broadly, happy. This friend, with whom I had long since lost touch, appeared in most of the photographs my mother had carefully arranged chronologically in the album I showed Andrew as I recounted my life.

He looked at me with wide eyes, his mouth ajar, as if listening to the most beautiful story. This attention made me blush and every now and then I would stop and look around the room, just to avoid his stare. I went out on the balcony and smoked a cigarette. He still had a depth in his gaze that made me unable to take my eyes off him, and his fleshy lips urged me to kiss him again. Still, I felt it wouldn't be wise.

I caught myself weighing my thoughts, afraid he might read them. We watched each other in silence, in a game of `who gives in first`, and I wasn't about to lose. It was a few moments, maybe hours, before I began to feel my soul grow weary. As if he already knew this, he grabbed my hand, and we stumbled off to the bedroom. His hand was frozen, and an almost morbid chill washed over me. For a moment, as he took my hand in his, the image of a peony-studded cavern flashed before my eyes. I tried to pull away, but an invisible force kept me there, in the crypt filled with my favorite flowers.

I could hardly bring my mind back to that unnatural present. It was very late when I discovered that everything around us had changed, it was already dark outside, and in the distance, I thought I could hear the sea singing. Although I was no longer looking at him, this handsome man's eyes were constantly on me. I felt his gaze just like a thousand arrows imbued with a sexuality that overwhelmed me. He wanted me. And I wanted him. Yet the feeling that I should be more restrained wouldn't give me peace.

A few hours later, like a nightingale, this beautiful mythical character was preparing to disappear, as the first rays of morning made their way through the curtains. He picked up his clothes and went to the bathroom, returning dressed and looking simply perfect. He kissed me on the forehead.

-       I will see you soon.

I was left alone in my rumpled bed, with a lost smile on my face and a splash of wine in the overturned bottle by the door.

After a few moments, I got out of bed and began to clean my room. Placing the photos back in the album, I noticed that the one taken in kindergarten, with all my classmates, was gone. Without paying much attention to this detail, thinking I would probably find it when I cleaned

...

A few days later, on a rainy Wednesday morning, I walked into the office, my hair curled from the humidity that had already lasted more than a week. It was not one of my good days. But as soon as I entered the office, I noticed a beautiful bouquet of peonies waiting for me on my desk. I was amazed and forgot I had my umbrella in my hand and it stumbled between my legs, causing a scene worthy of the laughing stunts - the coffee cup leapt out of my other hand and I went off balance, did a silly dance trying to right myself and mentally preparing for the moment of collision with the floor when, out of nowhere, I felt a strong arm break my fall.

- Dear Lord, how much disaster do you have in you, beautiful girl?

I looked him deep in the eyes and said:

- More than you can handle.
- That stands to be seen, Zozo. That's how the girls call you, right? Come on, go in your office and I'll bring you another coffee. There is something special waiting for you in there, Andrew said, winking. I picked them up myself, from my mother's garden.
- How did you know they were my favorites?
- I didn't know. They just seemed your style.

And with that he disappeared just as he'd appeared - without even knowing which direction he'd gone to or if I'd see him again soon, with the promised coffee. I clutched the bouquet, making sure no one saw my tender gesture towards the unexpected gift. Who the hell could understand this man... really.

Five minutes later he was reclining on the chair in front of my desk. He was sipping from a cup of coffee, watching circumspectly as I brewed mine.

- I cannot, for the life of me, understand how you can drink your coffee with so much sugar and still be healthy as a horse. No diabetes, no nothing.
- Just as I can't understand how your coffees are always so black and you drink them so often, yet you don't seem to have as dark a soul as their color.

He clutched his stomach with his hands and laughed heartily, even though my joke was neither very good, new, or even novel. He did that a lot - he laughed at my lines, genuinely, with a smile covering his entire face, which brightened my days more than I allowed myself to admit. He had a growing influence on me, though the mysteries surrounding him made me reluctant to approach him. Unfortunately for me though, I was already falling in love with him. And this man had the potential to cause me more pain than I could have imagined at the time.

Chapter 6

For three days I kept shaking from panic attacks that had already become too intense to bear, which is why I decided to ask for time off from work and stay indoors for a while to calm down. I didn't know what to do, and the thought that an attack could appear out of the blue at any moment made me, to my shame, provoke my own episodes. I suspected that it had all originated in a moment many years before this exhausting present in which I was trying to survive.

I must have been about 15 or 16. The moment I woke up shaken and hearing only my mother's desperate screams, I thought for a second that maybe I was still dreaming. I lied to myself that everything was fine and that in a few seconds I would wake up from the nightmare. I felt tiny shards pierce my hands and I remember seeing blood. The cold air hit my face with the force of a boxing glove, but I couldn't figure out where the cold was coming from. I was still in the car, that much I knew for sure.

Then I passed out. I had lost contact with the outside world and was at peace. I remember hearing such a soothing melody that I couldn't think of waking up from that sublime state. I was so calm. I could have sworn I was in heaven. My mother's desperate palm woke me up all too soon. The doctors said that if I had fallen into that state again, I wouldn't have woken up. Many times, I thought maybe it would have been better that way.

In the year after the accident, I kept lying to myself that everything was fine. I hid the painkillers under my pillow every time it was time for medication because everything was fine with me. I was fine. We were all fine, we were alive. I was breathing.

I said I could go back to school sooner than recommended. I lied to myself that my back pain and headache from the impact with the other car were temporary. I thought that the memory loss was normal. I continually lied to myself that I could get into a car without having a panic attack, even while I was having one, but never outwardly.

Looking back years later, I realized that maybe I had done it all too soon and was in too much of a hurry to get back to my old life. There are things in this life that you can do without fail, but you're afraid and tell yourself you can't. At the same time there are things that need to be done in their own time and you lie to yourself and insist you can do them faster.

Well, this moment would often sneak back into my thoughts, along with my mother's voice whispering in my ear: `You can't do it, you're too sensitive` or `Be careful, you know you're sick`. If at the beginning the anxiety would only surface at certain moments, I had finally come to the point where any stronger feeling, whether good or bad, brought me close to the abyss full of thoughts and terror. It was a very tiring way to live and sometimes I just wished I could turn it all off for a few moments. For the planet to sit still, for time to take a break and for me to be able to breathe. I was already realizing far too often that I was forgetting to take a deep breath, something so natural and yet so foreign to the person I'd become. I didn't recognize myself and I didn't know how to help myself, and the pain caused by all the thoughts that were grinding away at me, without being able to stop them, was unbearable.

And the most recent events hadn't helped me much either.

So, for three days I read, as much as I could, because my mind couldn't concentrate too much in one place and I often found myself turning many pages without having retained anything. In between, I'd allocate good hours to music. Anything I felt would calm me down was automatically added to the playlist. I smiled occasionally when a song reminded me of a happy moment but, more often than not, the songs found me in tears and left me feeling worse. I stared out the window, looking longingly at my neighbors, hoping to find something in their gestures that would help me hang on, catch my attention, and keep me from having panic attacks.

Instead, I finally managed to get my apartment organized. I assembled the kitchen furniture and placed each mug neatly on the hanging cupboard shelf, and each tea tin took its well-deserved place on the second shelf. I put the dishes in another cupboard as they came to hand, because I knew they had no chance of ever staying in order. I then cleaned out the fridge, only to realize that I didn't have much left in it once I threw out all the old stuff, and finally worked up the courage to try to eat a slice of toast with butter and tomatoes. During periods of heavy episodes, I found it very hard to keep anything down and would often stay hungry for days at a time.

After a few days of isolation, I finally felt a hint of normality. I was returning, shy and scared, to life. The first day back at work was the hardest, but it passed quickly and soon I was home again, covered in the thick duvet, looking out the window, and sipping hot tea. My cat was the happiest that I was home so much, and had been making the most of it. At all hours of the day and night he was where I was. In bed, in the kitchen or in the bathroom where, when I washed, he would sit on the edge of the sink and stare at me, as if he was making sure I wouldn't drown if he allowed himself to look away for a second.

...

I convinced myself to get out of the house for a bit and take a walk around the block, possibly go to the supermarket, and buy some food for me and Lale. Coming out of the flat, I bumped into a young, disheveled woman. She kissed my neighbor from the third floor, and he gently, reluctantly, peeled himself away from her and waved. Although I had only lived there for a few months, I was already getting used to his adventures. Every morning, on weekends, different women left his apartment, but all with the same look - first hopeful, then disappointed, as they realized that nothing was going to happen with this Don Juan who promised them in the night who knows what, only to say goodbye, carelessly, first thing in the morning.

I greeted him, disgusted, and continued my way down the stairs, behind the girl who had just left him. I knew she could feel my gaze on her, because she walked with her head bowed, clutching her bag to her chest, and with each floor she seemed to increase her pace in the hope that she would get out of my line of sight at some point. The truth was, I wasn't judging her. I had made her mistake at least once in my life, but the moment that helped me realize how embarrassing I was, was when I felt that exact same stare staring back at me. So, I continued to walk down quietly, my eyes fixed on the back of her head, until we were both out of the block and she turned left and I, even though I was supposed to be going in the same direction, chose to give her a slight head start and turned right.

Half an hour later I was back home with two large shopping bags, feeling strangely lighter than when I had left. I planned to bake a brownie to make up to Ileana and Ana the next day for missing so much from our rooftop gossip breaks.

Chapter 7

The next day I was back at the studio. The first man I saw was Andrew himself and for a few moments I felt my soul burning. I wasn't ready to meet him again, especially after the days I'd had. He saw me from the other end of the corridor and walked towards me, never taking his eyes off my face. Blood rushed to my cheeks, so I bowed my head a little to keep from giving myself away. When only a few steps were separating us, I looked up only to find, stunned, that he was preparing to walk past me as if we didn't know each other. My heart burned even more. I let him pass and stood still, my eyes fixating on the end of the hall from which he had come.

I thought maybe I had dreamed it all, just as I had dreamed it the first night after we met on my street. But how could a dream be so powerful that it made me think I had really lived it?

I finally managed get going and headed straight for the roof. I needed a breath of fresh air. It was raining outside. Although my first thought was to go back to the office and get my news ready for the next broadcast, my feet chose to guide me to the edge of the terrace. I lifted my face to the sky, and large drops of rain masked two tears that escaped the corners of my eyes and rolled down my cheeks.

All I could hear was the sound the rain made as it hit the railing, and it was so soothing that I stayed until my clothes were soaking wet and a little shiver pushed me inside.

- What the hell happened to you? Ileana asked and I didn't answer.

Ana immediately joined her. They each took me by one arm and guided me to their office. I got a big fluffy towel that had been washed with one of those balms that smell like spring. I started laughing. The girls looked at me partly startled, but then they started laughing too. A small puddle formed behind the chair, from the drips that trickled from my hair, straight onto the carpet. We continued laughing, like this, at everything and nothing at the same time, until our eyes locked on the same spot, and we suddenly stopped. Ana dared, in a low voice:

- Can we help you, Zoe? What's wrong with you? Where were you so many days and why are you soaking wet?
- Even I don't know how to help myself anymore, I told them both, vaguely smiling. I really didn't know what to do to start feeling warm again on the inside.

They both hugged me tightly and it was all I needed in that moment of uncertainty. I felt like I wanted to tell them what was going on, but I was afraid. `Maybe they'll understand, but what if they don't? I'm not ready to be without them`, I thought. I gave in to the embrace and closed my eyes. The puddle behind the chair was getting bigger and bigger, and Ili and Ana were laughing because I had wet their shirts too.

For the rest of the day, we kept it on the same note, mildly amused but also embarrassed - me because I'd scared them, them because they didn't understand. We went out for ice cream near the radio and let the sun kiss us, we even caught a rainbow and the girls each wanted an Instagram photo, so I proclaimed myself the group photographer. I didn't miss the sunset from the rooftop either. At the end of the day we said goodbye with another long, tight hug, and I slowly made my way home. I didn't want to be alone again. Not now.

...

Lale greeted me at the door, as usual, scolding me for being home late again.

-        Forgive me, you little snot.

I sat in the doorway on the cool floor, and he climbed into my arms, as he often did when he felt I was upset. I didn't let more than one more tear escape from the corner of my eye, and even that one

I quickly wiped away, as if I was afraid to show weakness even just in front of myself and Lale.

Soon I was in bed, under the duvet, with my knees drawn up to my chest. I turned on a random movie, which I didn't even watch. I just wanted some background sound so I could fall asleep. A few hours later though, tired but sleepless, I looked out my bedroom window and listened to the silence surrounding the neighborhood. I decided I would make a cup of coffee and wait on the balcony for the sun to rise, but not before lying in bed for at least another five minutes. I never made it to the kettle. I fell fast asleep and dreamed of Andrew. I woke up late, in the middle of a panic attack, not knowing how to calm down or who to call. I picked up my phone and almost dropped it when I saw the message waiting for me in the notification bar:

-    How are you?

He had sent me the message a few hours earlier, just after I had fallen back asleep, I suspected. I didn't know if or how to reply. `How am I doing? I'm not doing anything anymore`. I chose not to say anything. After all, he could walk past me as if I didn't even exist.

...

Over the next few days my phone filled up with messages and calls. Andrew insisted on talking to me, but I didn't want to. I was afraid to let him back in after he'd stepped on my very soul. He begged me in every message to give him a chance to make amends and explain everything that had happened. That is until one day when, leaving my apartment to go to work, I bumped into him. He had been waiting for me, for who knows how long, outside my door.

- I kept wanting to knock, but to be honest I didn't know what I would have said if you'd opened the door, how to begin, he started his monologue, with a faded smile in the corner of his mouth.
- `Hey, Zoe, I'm toxic`, how about you start with that? And we'll see where we go from there, I replied angrily and tried to get past him, but he grabbed me by the waist and pulled me to his chest.
- Please, Zoe... listen to me.

His gaze held me still and for a moment my anger faded. He was so handsome, with his curly brown hair that I wished I could run my fingers through over and over, and those sea-blue eyes that I often got lost in. He tried another smile because he knew I couldn't resist him when he did, but this time I surprised him. I couldn't smile back. He had disappointed me.

- What do you want, Andrew? I think you made yourself clear a few days ago in the newsroom lobby. I don't see what else we must talk about. I don't have time for this, I don't want cheap drama, and what I thought we might have, we don't. Is that what you wanted to tell me? Did you come up with some lame reason why you and I can't even say hello, let alone have anything together? I'm not interested in finding out. Why are you looking at me like that? I really don't...

But I didn't get to finish my big speech because his hard kiss stopped me midway through. I tried to resist, but he was holding my face in his hands, and I was so close to his body that I gave in. I wanted him as much as I felt, at that moment, that he wanted me. I pulled him into the apartment. For a few minutes I think I even forgot to breathe. There was nothing around. Just his gaze, fixed on me. Just me, in his embrace. A ray of light subtly swept over us, and the warmth penetrated us deeply. Just as, only moments before, his kiss had penetrated me to my very core.

It was raining lightly, and the first rays of sunshine that day were making their way through the clouds and reaching us. It was warm, and a scent of wine and oranges filled the room.

His hand rested so naturally on my thigh that for a moment I was convinced it had always been there. The dress I had long since lost somewhere in a dark corner of the room, and a subtle scent of lilac were the only reminders of the material he had so easily removed from my body.

My hands roamed his back as he clutched me to his chest and whispered, I don't know what... I had long lost track of time and there, next to him, it felt like years had passed and not just a few moments. It was so good and warm. We lost ourselves in each other's skin.

...

He left me naked and blushing, in my bed, and he leaned against the window. I watched him with lost eyes as he smiled and I gently touched my lips reddened from all the kissing. On my naked breasts he had left that scent I loved so much.

But then my dream was shattered. He took his clothes and began to dress, looked at me again for a long time, then urged me to do the same and go to work. I felt used up, drained of strength, and drained of all feeling.

I got up to get dressed but stopped halfway through. I watched him from the doorway as he took his black shirt off the floor and gently shook the traces of me off it. Along with them, he seemed to shake a bit of himself off onto the floor. I expected him to kiss me and leave, because I told him I wanted to stay and take a shower. I actually wanted to patiently gather in my thoughts his scent from the hallway and the love from the bedroom. Then I would carefully gather the shade from the window. I was going to lay them all on a bunch of lavender and store them in one of my mind's drawers, where I kept my fondest memories. I felt he was going to leave, not just then from my home, but forever from my life, and the traces of him would be the only ones that would bring me comfort.

He grabbed my hand, but I jerked away and tried to go to the other room. He wouldn't take no for an answer, so he came after me, grabbed my hand again and turned me to face him. He looked at me gently but seemed out of place.

- What is it, Andrew? What's the matter with you? Why do you keep running away?
- I'm sick, Zoe. It's serious. And how could I tell you that, tell you that I won't be able to be there for you as much as I'd like and as much as you deserve, knowing how you lost your brother? However, I couldn't resist the temptation of getting to know you better, of being close to you. I'm sorry.

- S... sick, was all I could manage, staring at him, waiting to see if he was joking.

I stayed pinned in place and felt like my legs were no longer listening to me. In the fall, Andrew grabbed me and held me in his arms, frightened. I didn't know how to react so, for the time being, I just chose to hug him tightly too. He was sick. How sick? Was there no cure for him? My soul broke into a thousand pieces, and I knew that there would be a time coming when, if he'd be gone, I would need serious treatment to heal from the sadness he would cause me. I didn't have the courage to ask him what the illness was, and he didn't seem very willing to open up. So, I chose to thank God that he was there, beside me, and that I could make him happy. I hoped that as time went on, he would be convinced that he didn't have to leave my side and that we would find a solution for this problem, whatever it was.

I stood up on his legs, and he reached behind my waist and began to move slowly from side to side. And I fell silent. And we watched each other like that, in silence, dancing, until the room was lightless, and we could no longer see each other. But we could hear our hearts beating to the beat of the song that would forever remain our favorite song - the one during which we truly found happiness for

the first time, in a place where everything was painted in black and
white.

Chapter 8

The next few days found us on my balcony, smiling at each other over the coffee table. He was reading and I was writing. I wanted to preserve as much of the authenticity of our moments together as possible. Mornings found us cuddling under the heavy duvet. He always made my coffee, because he said our moments in the newsroom kitchen would always be his favorite, and he wanted as many of them as possible. So, he would always make me tell him new things about myself before offering me the coffee mug as a prize, along with a tight kiss that made me sigh heavily.

In the evening, when I'd come into the house after a hard day, he'd undress me in the hallway, grab me by the waist and lead me into the bedroom, holding me tight to his chest. Then he'd lay me down on the bed and watch me. For a few minutes I wasn't allowed to say anything or react in any way, which I quickly learned. I watched him meekly as he lowered his eyes from my face down to my breasts, belly button and toes. Then he'd lean over me and start stroking my fingertips and kissing me until he felt me trembling with pleasure, begging him to penetrate me, to feel him close.

We made love until we were both tired. He would stay inside me, put his hands on my back and hold me tight so he could feel my body pressed against his. We were breathing shakily, but we were smiling and feeling our souls doing the same. I felt best there, next to his heart.

Then one day he left.

The morning I was left alone I woke up with a peony on his pillow and steaming coffee on my nightstand. I lay on the full length of the bed for a few minutes and peered out the window. The first rays of the morning were coming through the curtains and blinding me. I picked up the mug and took a sip of the perfect coffee Andrew had accustomed me to. I got out of bed and, on my way to the kitchen, stopped in the hallway and pinned my hair in a bun in front of the mirror next to the coat rack.

I put the peony in a glass of water and was getting ready to put something to eat when I saw it - a message, on a piece of paper stuck with a magnet on the fridge: `Until I get back, think about how I made you feel when I was here`. I thought of all the versions of where he'd left me, just like that, without so much as a last kiss, and in every version he'd come back.

Which is why I decided to spend the next weekend away from the city, at the river.

Chapter 9

I started my first morning in the company of the owner of the cottage I stayed at when I came here. It was a magical place where I would retreat to whenever I felt lost and wanted to find myself, and Lia knew that. So, she always welcomed me into her thin, trembling arms with a broad smile on her face.

- Welcome, my child, the old woman always said to me, as she placed a jug of wine between my palms and pressed her lips to my forehead, motherly.

I felt safe with Lia, as if she had been my mother in another life and we were destined to meet in this life as friends, in a cottage on the edge of a village long forgotten by the world.

The scenery was simply breathtaking, especially at sunset. This was also the reason why evenings always found me with my feet in the river, on the trail of the rays that ran from one end of it to the other, right by the cabin, before disappearing over the hill. The sun was so gentle that it seemed as if time stood still here, and the heat never left the river. The silence could get downright painful for those who lived for the noise of big cities, but for me it was therapeutic. Finally, after days, maybe months, of not having a moment truly to myself, I was dedicating two whole days to myself and to my beloved river. The murmur of the water always whispered the most beautiful stories to me, which I wrote down on paper. Then, when I would go back to the city and reread them, I would feel as if I had entered the world of another writer, because I couldn't believe that I'd had such inspiration.

-    Come on, put down the chisel and come to me, Lia shouted from the porch and woke me from my reverie.
-    Oh, no! What have I done, mother? I replied, laughing.
-    Come and see!

Without thinking too long, I closed the notebook and hurried back to the cottage, only to discover a veritable feast in the living room, on the coffee table in front of the fireplace - cheese, cold cuts, meatloaf, roast chicken, vegetable salad, melon, and a glass of wine for each of us. She always told me that only with me could she eat with gusto and joy, and I believed her. Because if she ate as much as she did when we were together, surely her placid construction would have long since been lost among waves and waves of fat.

I sat down in the armchair, my legs under me, rubbing my hands together with lust, which made Lia giggle. Nothing made her happier than the moments when guests gathered around the table and enjoyed her food. Although it was just the two of us now, the same wave of kindness and warmth washed over me as it did when we didn't have enough seats at the big kitchen table for all the guests.

After dinner, because it was still light outside, I went back to the river. I listened in fascination to the song of the water and the trees in the gentle breeze. A few rays of sunlight crept through the branches and caressed me in passing, trying to reach the river and go for a swim. There was such a deep stillness I hadn't felt in so long that I'd forgotten how much I needed it.

It was hours before I realized that the sun had long since set and I couldn't see to read. I lit the lantern Lia always put in my picnic basket before I left.

...

The lantern story was almost as old as our friendship. I might even say that old Lia had saved my life, in one of my first summers at the cabin. I wanted to go out for the night and discover the village at a walk. But she was worried.

- Be careful, child, if you get caught at night in the village, it's not a very pleasant atmosphere. At least take this lantern with you, and if you find yourself on a dark alley, light it. Don't joke about darkness in this village.

- Lia, don't worry, nothing will happen to me, I said and took the lantern in my left hand while my right hand I raised to her, instead of `goodbye`.

I was already with my back to the cabin when I heard her say again, this time more to herself, `Be careful, child...`.

It wasn't long before I was lost in the village, for though it was small, the streets were pretty damn winding. Whichever decision I made, whichever street I walked down, I would always turn around in front of the hut from which, from the early hours of the morning, men's voices were echoing, and clinking pints of beer and glasses of brandy could be heard. This village, full of drunks and low lives, was like a labyrinth from which I didn't know how to get out. And when the clock in the village church tower announced 11 PM, Lia's words echoed in my mind like a broken tape: `Be careful, child...`. I took many rights, then took a left. Then another left and another right. And so on, until finally I hit a dark street, exactly what the old lady had told me to avoid. I looked for the matchbox in my jacket pockets, then, with growing concern, in my jeans' pockets. When I found it in one of the back pockets, a little yelp, half panic, half joy, escaped me and shrouded the darkness. I quickly lit the lantern.

In the candle flame, a grotesque figure appeared to me. It was one of the men from the pub, I assumed, because the smell of alcohol came out through all his pores. He didn't even have to open his mouth. But he did. And when the few teeth he had left, one yellow, the rest decayed or broken, were framed in a wide smile, I knew it was time to run. The hideousness, however, grabbed me by the jacket and pulled me back. He hugged me so tightly that for a moment I felt like he could do anything he wanted to me; he was so strong. I turned to him and looked him straight in his glassy with alcohol eyes. When his dirty hand slipped into my jeans, while the other still held me against his chest, everything went dark before my eyes. I could hear a loud screech in the back of my head. Whether it was panic or a momentary glare, I don't know, but my hand jerked out of his grip and the lantern hit him square in the head. He let go of me shocked and screaming in pain.

I took off, running, and as if by magic I found the right way to the river. I didn't look back until I reached the cabin. Lia was reading on the porch when I arrived, and I jumped right into her arms. It was the only time the village caught me on my own, in the evening, on the labyrinthine streets.

...

The two days at the riverside cottage were just what the doctor had ordered - I read incessantly, watched the sunset, sipped from a steaming coffee at sunrise, with Lia to my right. I laughed a lot and talked even more. I told her about Andrew and how wonderful it could all be, but also about the mysterious illness he was suffering from. Lia let out a deep sigh and hugged me as only she knew how - with a mother's love and the strength of a thousand sisters. She knew Lucas's story and how much I was still suffering.

- You will come here, she told me, and I will take care of your soul. We will take away your pain, me and your beloved river.

Chapter 10

Autumn was struggling to get into its stride, after a summer that was still stubbornly bringing high temperatures to the city, when my colleagues came up with the idea of a team building in the middle of nature, in the mountains. I wanted to go to the sea. Because I got Ileana and Ana on my side, and Andrew said from the start that we would do whatever I wanted, convincing the rest of them was a piece of cake. In a few days everything was ready, the bags were packed, the reservations were made. We had rooms at a hotel by the sea, for which I suspected my boss had paid quite a lot, which meant the newsroom was doing well.

On the day I left, Andrew came by my apartment to pick up my bags and then followed me to the newsroom - I had some writing to do and didn't want to leave it to someone else. I wanted to make the most of this long-awaited trip, my first one with him. He put his hands on my shoulders and looked at me smiling, but pretending to be embarrassed:

- You really couldn't help yourself, could you?
- You know me, I would have sat and stressed for two days straight if I hadn't finished that newsletter. It was my

responsibility; I didn't want to leave it on someone else's shoulders.

He laughed out loud, nodding disapprovingly.

- Just like I said: you couldn't help being perfect! Are you trying to impress me? Don't you know you already have?
- But do you know I love you?

The words came out of my mouth so naturally, so unexpectedly, that they startled me. I couldn't remember the last time I'd said that to someone or how those two words had made me feel. All I knew was that now it felt good to have said it, even though I'd been the first in the relationship to do it, even though he might not have felt the same way, even though he might die, and I didn't know when.

- I love you, I found myself telling him again. Does that scare you?

He took my face in his hands, as he often did before he left, kissed me tightly and looked at me for a few moments, saying nothing. I felt the blood rush to my cheeks and the tears were getting ready to spill, so I tried to look away, but he wouldn't let me.

He kissed me one more time, then let me go and turned back to the car to open the door for me. I got in, trying to meet his gaze, but he didn't look my way again. Instead, I managed to catch him, in the rear-view mirror, as he walked to the trunk to drop off another bag, quickly wiping away a tear.

He drove the whole way without a word. He was smug and I knew better than to disturb him from the moment he had with himself, so I kept quiet too. I chose instead to place my left hand on the one he was resting on his shifter. He flinched, as if he wasn't used to such touches. As if he'd forgotten what it felt like to have someone hold your hand. But instead of withdrawing his hand, he looked at me for a second and let his fingers curl through mine. Then he squeezed harder like he wanted to make sure it was real, that I was there.

...

We were the last to arrive at the hotel. The rest of my colleagues were still outside, waiting for their rooms to be prepared. Ana and Ili were caught up in an intense conversation. It was the first time I had seen Ana so engaged and she even seemed a little upset. Ileana was rolling her eyes and refuting every argument her friend made. I preferred not to get into their argument, because I was sure that whatever the problem was, they would solve it quickly and without my help.

A few steps away from the girls stood Marcus, my boss, and I was glad to finally see him in shorts and a t-shirt. He never shed his always pressed suits, and I resented that, because those who didn't know him the way I did, thought he was one of those rich guys who would do anything to succeed. Marcus was far from this impression, he left on strangers. I had seldom met a man with such warmth. He was always interested in the welfare of his employees and often gave up his few hours off so that someone else could have a break to deal with their personal problems. Whenever I had bad days with panic attacks, he was the first to know and the first to urge me to go home. He knew I didn't want to talk on the phone at those times, so he preferred to leave me a message every few hours, just to remind me that he was there if I somehow needed something or finally wanted to talk to someone.

- Marcus, you look very well among the earthlings!
- You're funny, Zoe, he replied, pretending to be serious, but a smile that blossomed in the corner of his mouth gave him away.
- What finally convinced you to choose the sea?

-    Look at them, he said, and I followed the hand he held out to his colleagues. Look how happy they are to be here. You did that. If we'd gone to the mountains, as I insisted, we wouldn't have had the waves and the sun and the warm sand and this view. Maybe they wouldn't have been so happy either and I certainly wouldn't have been in shorts.

I laughed heartily at his remark about pants and his sad play-pretend look, then patted him on the shoulder, a gesture he often did when he wanted to show closeness to someone without wrinkling his jacket in a hug.

We all sat on the hotel terrace until the rooms were ready and, a little out of boredom, a little from too much heat, decided to order a round of beers. Then another one and two more after that. And just like that, a few hours later the terrace was echoing with the noise coming from our table as the sun was preparing to set.

Andrew beckoned me to the beach and headed that way. I followed him immediately, but for part of the way I kept a few steps back. My confession and his reaction were still too vivid in my mind for me to be able to be too close to him. After a few minutes he turned to me, annoyed.

- Come here. What's this? I never want to see you anywhere but to my right, he said and grabbed my hand, seriously.

I dropped my gaze to the ground, and we walked the rest of the way to the beach in silence. I wanted to take it back.

On the shore he stopped suddenly and, without looking at me, let go of my hand. A wave reached my feet. I turned to Andrew and scrutinized him. He was gorgeous. A man any woman would want. But there he was with me, on the shore, his hands as cold as a grave and a scent that made me forget the unpleasantness of the situation. I kissed him. Briefly. Like I'd been doing this my whole life with him.

We stripped down to our underwear and quietly entered the water. It was already dark, and our only landmark was the moon. The water, warm at first, got colder as we went along. `Stay`, he said in a choked, whispered voice. Instinctively, I tried to pull away and reach the shore. His hand, now heavy, held me so tightly, however, that I could do nothing but surrender to his power. He embraced me and I plunged into the depths, and this love, so unexpected, so beautiful and cold at the same time, held me so tight that I could do nothing but embrace it and forget where I had come from and where I was going...

I lost my underwear in the sea that night, a good reason for Andrew to have a good laugh at my expense. I laughed with him too, lovingly hugging him and berating him for being the one who had undressed me, so the blame for the nakedness in which I was forced out of the water lay with him. He offered me his shirt and it was long enough to reach almost to my knees, so we wandered around the resort at leisure until dawn.

...

We walked into the hotel room still laughing, his arm resting around my shoulders. I freed myself from his grasp and threw myself onto the bed, letting my body hide among the white sheets. Andrew followed me. He pretended he was going to throw himself on top of me and I screamed briefly. He laughed, then gently sat on top of me and I was so happy under his weight that our laughter turned to smiles and the stillness of the morning swept the room. He rested his head on my shoulder sighing and whispered something.

-     What did you say? I asked puzzled.

-     Nothing. Nothing.

-     Come on, tell me, I insisted with a pleading voice.

He leaned on his hands and moved closer to my face so that there was only room between our lips for a ray of sunshine. He took a deep breath.

-    I said, `I love you`. I love you, Zoe.

Even though I knew I didn't need to, I repeated the same thing to him. We spent the rest of the day locked in our room, in bed, with him on top of me, resting his head on my chest. I slept soundly that night, and so did he.

The next morning, I was to learn what it means to love and lose everything in a single second.

Andrew was not waking up, and his hands were colder than ever. For a moment I was sure I was going to have another panic attack, but I managed to calm down enough to think clearly and look for a solution to help him. Not knowing what else to do, I called an ambulance.

The waiting was driving me crazy and I was torn between trying to hear his heart beat and some indicative that the ambulance was near. In what seemed like an eternity of waiting, I tried to stay calm and kept telling him I loved him, as if I was sure my words would somehow save his life. Finally, the ambulance arrived, and a rescuer knocked on the door. I felt as if it was God himself in the doorway. I welcomed him into the room with tears in my eyes and all I could say to him was `please save him. it took me a lifetime to find him`.

The monitor that had been strapped to his heart barely managed to register a heartbeat, until suddenly it didn't register anything. That sound would haunt me for a long time, especially in the nights to come.

Paramedics struggled to resuscitate him. They were whispering to each other, as if I wasn't there, as if I was just a ghost... and that was exactly how I felt. I couldn't conceive that there was a life in which he didn't live, in which I couldn't stroke his cheek and see his sweet smile in the morning. It was by far one of the most traumatic moments of my life. Little did I know it was about to get a lot worse.

They managed to resuscitate him, after too long, and they were wondering if he would have any brain activity after waking up. So, I stood by his side, praying, asking God, the Universe, any higher force that would be listening, to save him.

And then he opened his eyes. He was looking at me with a lost gaze, as if he wasn't even there.

- Say something, please, anything, I kept telling him, with no answer to come.

Until, finally, he managed to say:

- You know that if we stay together this is bound to happened again, right?
- If you always come back to me and don't go to the light or what the hell happens if you die, it's ok with me. I'd rather have a scare, than a lifetime without you.

He kissed me and I felt his lips finally warm up, so, exhausted but peaceful, I fell back asleep and for the rest of the day I didn't get out of bed.

…

We spent the rest of the holiday on the beach with our colleagues, enjoying the rustling of the water and the breeze that caressed us as we lay under the umbrella, watching in amusement as the rest of them ran around like children or swam until the sun went down. I would look worriedly at Andrew every time he seemed to lose his smile or get up with difficulty, and he would always laugh back at me:

- I'm not a crystal ball, baby. I'm not going to break. I'm just a little tired, it's normal, we're at sea. You know what fresh air does to me. I'd like to sleep non-stop if I could. But I'm fine,

I'm all right, I couldn't put you through that scare again, I promise.

- Okay, fine, let's say I believe you, I told him, rolling my eyes and trying my best to smile as wide and encouraging as possible.

Because I most likely couldn't convince him that I was calmer, he grabbed my hand and held me tight until we left the beach.

Two days later, we were heading back home and I couldn't help but glance in the rear-view mirror at the sea. I wished I could have stayed there for the rest of my life. Together with Andrew, whom I had childishly tried to convince that the sea would cure him of everything and keep him forever young, I would surely have led the life I had always dreamed of.

- We could open a café by the sea!
- We could, yes.
- And have books in it, and Lale could walk around freely, be among people, you know how he loves that.
- I know, Zoe.
- And you could work there with me. And in our spare time we'd go to the seashore and tell stories to the beautiful Sea.

He looked at me from time to time and laughed at my stories, but I could feel my plans inspiring him. Maybe if we had more time, maybe if he was healthy, maybe...

When we got home, Andrew dropped me off at my apartment and promised we would see each other soon. He had a few things to take care of. Without giving much thought to what he'd told me, though something made me think I should have insisted he stay with me, I let him go and went into the apartment. I still felt like walking out to the balcony quickly and watching him as he headed back to his house, just as I had the first night we spent together.

Chapter 11

A short knock let me know there was someone at the door. I got out of bed without much enthusiasm and looked out the peephole but saw no one. At first, I thought one of the kids on the block was playing pranks again and took a few steps back towards the bedroom. Then, as if in a dream, a voice whispered to me to turn around and open the door, which I did.

Waiting for me in the doorway was a white envelope with no name or stamp, a plain envelope that incited my curiosity. I picked it up from the door's wiper, then studied it in the light coming through the large staircase window, as if trying to see through it. I closed the door behind me and with a knife, in one swift movement, stripped the letter of its wrapping. A faint hint of perfume hit me, and I knew. Andrew.

I let the paper fall from my hand to the floor and collapsed beside it. No. It couldn't. Not him. In the envelope were two photos, the one that had disappeared from my album and another, identical to the first.

Gradually, the sun's rays loosened their embrace and gave way to a breeze that woke me from my trance. I looked up at the open balcony door. It was already dusk, and I was still on the floor, clutching my knees and the letter to my chest. I couldn't bring myself to open it, because once I did, I knew it would all be over. It would be true. Finally, after what seemed like an eternity, Lale approached me purring and looking at me circumspectly. I held out my hand and tried for a smile, and he made his way onto my lap, telling me in his own way that he was here for me, that I could read Andrew's last words. And so, I did.

" Zoe...

I have so many things I'd like to tell you, but I'll start with the best of them - the reason we felt a special closeness to each other is in the photos I left for you in the envelope. When you showed me your album, this photo vaguely brought back brief moments from my childhood... including the existence of a duplicate of the photograph somewhere in my mother's memories. So, when I left town for a few days, I stopped by my parents' house to convince myself that I was right. My mother knew exactly where to look and immediately showed me the same picture, with many happy faces of kindergarten children gathered around Santa Claus. She showed me which of the little ones was me, then she showed me the one I proudly called my sweetheart - it was you.

I told you I had been curious about you for a long time, longer than I let on. That's because I'd noticed you even before you moved into your new apartment near my house. And even then, I felt I should know you, be close to you somehow. Which is what happened, the first time on my initiative, when we met on your street, the second time on the Universe's plan. My heart stopped when you entered the radio building and I saw you in the kitchen for the first time, looking for the coffee that fate had placed in my arms at that very moment.

Now that I've told you all this, you're probably wondering even more why I'm leaving these lines written down for you instead of telling you directly - because as much as I'd like to always be with you, I can't do that, baby. I can't put my happiness above your right to lead a fulfilled life with happiness and a love that won't leave you because of a wretched disease that is ripping more and more out of me with each passing day.

Please forgive me for leaving. I know I promised to take care of you, and it may not seem like it, but I am. I'm trying to find my words, to somehow explain to you why this is happening, but I can't find anything. So, I'm doing the one thing I shouldn't be doing - shutting up.

I'm defective. I know, you would tell me now, smiling, that we are all flawed and that our flaws complement each other, but I don't believe that. I think I would break your soul in my hands while trying to protect it. And your soul has already been through too much to endure another trauma.

I want you to know that I'm not doing so good myself. It's not easy for me to stay away from you, knowing that when you close your eyes at night, your tears come uncontrollably. Don't tell me it isn't so because I know you.

Please forgive me, but I know that if I saw you, I couldn't help but take your face in my hands again. I'd kiss you long and hard and I don't think I could let you go. We'd practically start over and I couldn't stay with you. I go round and round trying to understand, to be able to somehow explain to you why I'm letting go of your hand when all I want is to wake up every morning, look at your smile and prepare your coffee. It's better that way for you. You'll suffer less.

Remember our first night together, when I told you I saw something special in you. Know that was the moment I knew that if we stayed together, I would love you as I've never loved anyone before.

Maybe you're already bored with reading this, but I promise it won't be long before I'm done. I'm trying to come up with an ending, but nothing feels right. How can I say goodbye when all I want is for you to be with me always? I know. I'm stupid. My head is spinning. I should run to you and tell you how I feel.

Please forgive me. Please try to understand for me because I don't know how or why all this happened. I won't forget you. I hug you the same way I hugged you the last time we were good. Remember that and nothing else. Remember that I wish I had time to love you. "

I hid under the heavy duvet and closed my eyes. I tried to remember Andrew's every feature - the mole on his neck, the twinkle in his eyes where I could always see the sea, his fingers hardened from working in the workshop where he spent his spare time creating wooden objects. I already missed him and when I tried to let all these feelings come out, I felt like I was choking and suddenly stopped. I couldn't bear the wave of despair and grief that hit me every time I allowed myself to begin to understand that he wasn't coming back.

His last words sang in my mind afterwards all night. `Remember I wish I had time to love you...` like a broken tape, was all

I could hear for hours, until finally the sun rose again, sending its rays to caress my tear-reddened cheeks tenderly.

That morning I got out of bed as if nothing had happened. I couldn't feel all the pain anymore, so I chose, for a brief moment, to feel nothing, to forget, to live in a present where his letter didn't exist. I hid it in the freezer, hoping that once his words had frozen, so would the love I had for him.

I looked at myself in the large mirror in the hallway and smiled, then set off to work, thinking I would never meet him again in the newsroom kitchen, clutching the coffee pot tightly to his chest.

...

Arriving at the newsroom, I stopped in front of the building, as I had done on my first day of work. Just as then, this time I was again afraid of the unknown. I couldn't know what my life would be like without being close to Andrew after all this time. I was numb. Rooted in the cement in front of the building. Gripped by a longing that would become more painful before it could become bearable.

I turned around and called Marcus to tell him I wasn't feeling well and needed a few days off.

- Honey, I saw you from my office window. It's okay. Please, take all the time in the world. We'll still be here when you want to come back. Or if you want to talk to someone, you know I'm not just a boss in a suit.
- Thank you, Marcus. All I need to do is turn the clock back and stop it. Guess no one can help me with that... so I'll be back as soon as I can.

I went back in the car and drove off to nowhere, trying to clear my head before heading home.

Chapter 12

I took a healthy gulp of air and started desperately kicking my feet. The door wouldn't budge an inch. I knew I was going to die. I could already feel it in every pore.

It only took a second... I wanted to somehow stop the pain that was stabbing in my chest like a sword. So, I simply set off, with one of his favorite songs blaring. I was driving down the valley road, with no destination in mind, when out of nowhere, a deer came flying at me, so I jerked the wheel, trying to avoid the impact. The car took off towards the river and the next thing I knew, water was rushing into my panic-stricken lungs.

Then it was all like a dream. I remembered my mother and father, Andrew, Ana, Ileana. At that moment, as I floated in the cold, dirty river water, I hesitated only for a second. I closed my eyes and gave up. One second. A second that would cost a life.

After a sleep that seemed to last too long, I woke up. I was still here. I started punching doors, screaming, choking, the panic taking hold of me until... I saw myself. Peaceful, serene, as if deep in a restful sleep, I lay in the water. Then a distorted face appeared at my window.

I'm saved`, I thought for a second, and again started to kick my feet and show the rescuer that I was there. But silence fell over us again, over me and her, the dead one, lying there soulless and not letting me save her, and from the window smiled at me this time the gentle and beautiful face of my brother.

...

When I saw the car plunging into the water, somehow, I knew it was going to end there. I admit, for a second I felt liberated.

As I watched my body float away, I turned back to Andrew. I imagined his hand grabbing me in the darkness of the night and saving me. I heard him say `I love you` and `Fight for us`. For a few minutes it was enough for me to try again to wake up from this nightmare.

I wonder how was he going to react when he found out I was gone? That I wasn't breathing? No longer feeling? Was he still alive, or had he left just so he could die in peace? Was I going to see him again once I had taken my last breath?

It was dark and I was a little afraid. `You know I've never liked being alone...much less in the dark`, I said to him, the one in my memories. I wish someone could have lit a little light for me. I tried to light something in the car, but my hands were running across the dashboard. Does death mean a total darkness where you can see your body lying there, and nothing you can do about it?

I had already forgotten how long I had been lying there and felt my flesh swelling on me. I think I read somewhere once, or maybe someone told me, that when you drown, if the water isn't too cold, your flesh swells up on you. I wished he'd remember me beautiful, without the traces of the river soaked into the skin of a woman who died in a stupid accident.

...

Funny thing about death, too. You're born, without having asked for it. Then you struggle a lifetime to stay alive. The days pass you by and you fight against the Time that stubbornly makes you older with every second. They were probably going to say I died in an accident. No one would have ever believed that I wanted to take my own life. I didn't, between you and me. But now, as the water enveloped me in the embrace that I had asked for in everyone's eyes but received too few of, I decided that this dirty, cold water would be the one to hold me tightly in its arms, to make all the pain and panic attacks and anxiety go away.

I waltzed with death, and it was beautiful.

But did I really want to die? I saw, with my mind's eye, a little girl smiling at me, as her frail little hands reached out. A little child was growing inside me, a tiny human for whom I was to be everything, whom I had to protect, for whom I had to survive... with my last strength I began to flail and search for the power to hold on until someone would save me. Then everything suddenly went black.

We met at the radio. But I'd been fond of her for a long time. She didn't know it, but I often saw her walking through the park near the neighborhood where I lived, and once she even passed the building where I worked. I saw her from the balcony where I'd usually spend my breaks. I still remember how beautiful she was, even from a distance. That day she had a long, white dress on, made of some sort of material that made her look like a bride.

- What a woman, I remember saying to myself at the time, captivated by the lightness with which she walked, as if she were floating, and the curls that, in the breeze, caressed her face.

Always when I saw her, she looked thoughtful, as if all the weight of the world had rested on her shoulders, and I woke up every time wishing I could take the wrinkles in her forehead with my fingertips and carry all her troubles, just to see her smile. I knew that if I came into her life, I wouldn't be helping her, but only adding weight to her flat figure. However, I couldn't help it... I was curious about her and what was hidden in her soul. What was it that made her seem so sad sometimes when I saw her?

One day I was surprised to see her in my neighborhood. She had come out of one of the new blocks on the street parallel to the one my house was on, and I couldn't resist the temptation to approach her. We passed each other, seemingly by chance, and our hands touched lightly. In that moment I felt how much love my soul could have had for this woman whose name I used to dream of finding out and whisper it in her ear, as I held her in my arms. I marveled at how many hidden desires I discovered with each extra moment I spent thinking of her...

Sooner than I had ever dared to desire, I met her. She stepped into the newsroom kitchen, reaching for the coffee pot, with such naturalness that I felt the Universe had sent her to me and told me it was time to take care of her. Which I did, for as long as I could, without allowing myself to realize, however, that once I inevitably left her life, Zoe would be left with an extra weight on her shoulders - that of having carried a once-in-a-lifetime love for a man who would not live long enough to receive all that love.

I was suffering from some sort of a cardiomyopathy that put me in danger of going into cardiac arrest. It was not pretty; I can tell you that. And believe me when I tell you I didn't want anyone to know or to have to go through this with me. So then why would I want to enter this woman's life when, with each passing day, I was getting weaker and weaker, and the treatment didn't seem to be working. The doctors had already told me repeatedly that I was going to die soon and that I should get used to the thought and put an end to my unresolved problems, say goodbye to my loved ones, accept it... but how could I accept that I would not be able to live the rest of my life with the woman I knew was my destiny?

...

After a few months with her, Zoe showed me a photo album from her childhood. My already weakened heart almost stopped when I noticed a photo identical to one I'd seen at home, among the pictures my mother kept in the library. Because I didn't want to tell her all this without being sure, I slipped the photo into my sweatshirt pocket when Zoe wasn't paying attention and headed home to my folks as soon as I could. I had to know.

My mother was beyond thrilled when she found out my love story. As much as I tried to explain to her that it wasn't going to be a story with a happy ending, she just wouldn't accept that I was going to die. Consequently, she was already making plans and even the menu for when I would bring Zoe to meet my family. My heart wouldn't let me argue with her, so I played along.

- I think she'd rather have the sausages, Mom, instead of those fancy dishes you keep talking about. She's a simple girl. That's why I love her.

- Gosh, child, I never thought I'd have the joy of seeing such a twinkle in your eye. I'll cook anything she wants for the one who's made you so happy. You've changed so much, my mother said, stroking my cheek as she had done since I was a child, when I did something right.

She looked for the album in question, knowing exactly where the photo I was referring to was hidden. It was the same one I had stolen from Zoe's photos, but I didn't remember much from that time, so I asked my mother if she remembered anything. It didn't take her long to make the connection between my girlfriend and a little girl with long dark hair, smiling broadly from the photo, while holding hands with a boy with sea-colored eyes.

- You were telling everyone that she was your future wife, that you would be with her all your life. I laughed at the time, because I never thought that bonds formed at such a young age could stay alive. But it's her, Andrew. I remember now. You'd call her Zozo, and she'd always laugh with her mouth up to her ears, then hug you with her little hands. You were inseparable. After a year, she moved with her family to another part of the city, so they moved her out of kindergarten too, and I didn't keep in touch with her parents. I had only heard that Zoe's father had left the country, without knowing why.

- She had a brother, Mom. Lucas. He died when Zoe was still young, and her father couldn't bear the pain and left to work abroad. She was left with just her mother for a while. So, you tell me, how can I still be with her, knowing what she went through? Knowing how much she suffered when her brother died, sick? I'm selfish.
- You're in love! I'm sure you don't have a selfish cell in your body. Is she happy with you?
- Yes. At least she seems to be. I love her with all my heart, and I don't know what to do, I don't know if she'd be better off with me or without me. What should I do, Mother? Tell me, please.
- Love her, son. That's all you can do for her. Love her as you want her to love you. Love her as much as you can, all her life, or at least until... until...

And she couldn't go on. She burst into tears and hugged me tight.

...

I had one last attempt to find a chance at recovery, a miraculous cure that would give me hope for life. I had heard of a doctor who specialized in my condition, but it was a day's drive to him. I took a few days off and promised Zoe I'd be back, without telling her where I was going. I didn't want to get her hopes up. In fact, I didn't want to get my hopes up in the first place.

I was about to find out that this doctor was working on a treatment dedicated to more serious cases, just like mine. But he couldn't promise me it would be ready to administer before I ran out of time.

- Your case is advanced. If it was at an early stage, you would have had more time to wait for my treatment. Unfortunately, however, I don't know when I will be ready to offer it to the patients, the doctor confessed, patting me on the back, visibly saddened.

At that moment, all the plans I had foolishly made for Zoe and myself died. I decided, however, that I would spend the last part of my life with her, whether it lasted a few more months or a few more years, at best. I took her to the sea because I knew how much she wanted it.

As the days went by, I felt worse and worse. My hands were getting colder, and every morning it became progressively harder to get out of bed. I was weak and dizzy, and my heart was pounding, as if every step I took was a marathon. I tried to conceal it, but often Zoe would see something that made her worry - the colorless cheeks, the dry, cold lips, the weakened body that I barely turned towards her at times.

After I almost died on our seaside holiday, I decided I didn't want her to remember me for the rest of my life as the wreck I was soon to become. I left. Like a coward, I left her alone, not even having the strength to say goodbye to her as she deserved. And it was the hardest thing I'd ever done in my entire life, and one I would regret forever.

...

When I saw her lying helpless on the hospital bed, I cried like a baby. I fell to my knees beside her bed and squeezed her cold hand in mine. I spent days sleeping on the armchair I had convinced a nurse to put in Zoe's room, just so I could be always near her. Time was passing, but she wasn't waking up from her coma.

- She was pregnant when she crashed, I was told when I got to the hospital. Unfortunately...

But I couldn't hear what they told me next, a ton of medical terms I didn't care about. Zoe could have had someone in her arms after I was gone, a soul to hold on to with all her strength when she missed me the hardest. I had done that. I was to blame for her lost life and the pain she would feel when she found out. I had single-handedly destroyed the last shred of light that struggled to shine from her body, shadowed by the burdens she always carried on her shoulders. I wasn't surprised she didn't wake up. After all, what could she possibly want to live for...

I left the salon to answer the phone. It was my doctor. The treatment was ready. He could give it to me if I wanted. I could have a new chance at life, but I wouldn't have wanted it if she hadn't been there for me.

I ran to her room and collapsed back to the side of the bed, desperate. She had to come back to me. She had to!

- Zoe, please wake up. Come back to me. We can finally be happy. We'll go to the sea; you'll have everything you ever wanted and more. I can heal. There's a cure that can save me, but I don't want to do it without you. I can't do this without you, baby, please. Forgive me for all the pain you've felt because of me, let me make it up to you, let me carry the burden on your shoulders for the rest of your life.

I stayed by her bedside, holding her hand, hoping that I could thus give her the little willpower she needed to gain strength and wake up. Then, as if in a dream, it seemed to me that she squeezed me back.

I looked up.

Her eyes were open.

Index